AF444663

Women in the Apostolic Move

Elder Rochella O'Quinn

McClure Publishing, Inc.

Rochella O'Quinn © Copyright 2022

All rights reserved. Printed and bound in the United States of America. According to the 1976 United States Copyright Act, no part of this book may be reproduced or utilized in any form or by any means, electronic or mechanical, including photocopying, recording, or by any information storage or retrieval system, except by a reviewer who may quote brief passages in a review to be printed in a magazine or newspaper, without permission in writing from the Publisher: Inquiries should be addressed to McClure Publishing, Inc. Permissions Department, 398 West Army Trail Road, Bloomingdale, IL 60108. First Printing: April 30, 2022.

Scripture quotations are taken from the HOLY BIBLE, KING JAMES VERSION, Cambridge, 1769. Public Domain.

THE HOLY BIBLE, NEW INTERNATIONAL VERSION®, NIV® Copyright © 1973, 1978, 1984, 2011 by Biblica, Inc.® Used by permission. All rights reserved worldwide.

Scriptures marked NKJV are taken from the NEW KING JAMES VERSION (NKJV): Scripture taken from the NEW KING JAMES VERSION®. Copyright© 1982 by Thomas Nelson, Inc. Used by permission. All rights reserved.

ISBN-13: 979-8-9853967-4-4

Cover Design by Kathy McClure

To order additional copies, please contact:
McClure Publishing, Inc.
www.mcclurepublishing.com
800.659.4908

Acts 2:17-18

In the last days, God says, I will pour out my Spirit on all people ... even on my servants, both men and women.

(NIV)

In the last days saith God, I will pour out of my Spirit upon all flesh..., and on my servants and my handmaidens.

(KJV)

Table of Contents

Introduction
Women in the Apostolic Move

Joel 2:28-29; Acts 2:17-18

Are you a woman wondering where you are in God's apostolic move? Where do you fit in with what He is doing right now? This manual will give you insight into your role as a woman in God's apostolic assignment in the earth and where your place is in this movement.

Before, during, and after Jesus being here on the earth, women had key roles in His life and ministry. We will look into the lives of Hannah, Esther, Priscilla, and Deborah in the areas of prayer, deliverance, evangelism and the prophetic.

In the last days, God says He will pour out His Spirit on all people even on His servants, both men and women. (NIV) Part of the last days is the restoring of the apostolic (apostle) in the body of Christ to help prepare the way for the second coming of Christ.

In the next seven lessons, we will discuss the apostolic movement, the woman's role in it, apostolic attributes of prayer, deliverance, evangelism and the prophetic. Last, but certainly not least, twenty-first century examples of women as Apostles.

Scripture references are included for your own personal study, mediation, and reflection as such the Bible tells us in Acts 17:11 to search/examine the scriptures to see if what is said is true. I have referenced throughout this book the King James Version (KJV) and New International Version (NIV); please use whatever version of the Bible that is best for you.

Objective: The role that women have in the apostolic move

    I.   Apostolic (Apostle): Ephesians 4:11-12

        a. Definitions - what it is and what it is not

        b. Purpose - restoration of the five ascension gifts

        c. Attributes of the Apostolic - there are many, but we will discuss a few in detail:

            i. Prayer and Deliverance

            ii. Evangelism and Prophetic

    II.   Women - What is her role in the Apostolic?
           Galatians 3:28

a. God's purpose and plan for Women

b. God does not discriminate and does not have respect of persons

c. My (personal) position in God being made clear, and I am being molded by God into it

III. Apostolic Attribute: Power through Prayer
I Samuel 1:10, 12-15

a. Hannah as an example

i. Travailing prayer

ii. Manifestation from that prayer

b. The importance of prayer for the Apostolic move

c. My prayer life has intensified, strengthened, and elevated to new level

IV. Apostolic Attribute: Deliverance – Esther –
Esther 4:14

a. Esther operating in obedience and authority

b. The role of deliverance in the Apostolic

c. Power of deliverance has become more real to me, learned how to war in the spirit

V. Apostolic Attribute: Evangelism – Priscilla
Acts 18:18, 24-28

a. Priscilla as an example; team ministry – co-laborers with Apostle Paul

b. Spreading the Gospel (Good News) of Jesus Christ - our Great Commission

c. Becoming more Kingdom minded and soul conscious

VI. Apostolic Attribute: Prophetic
Ephesians 2:19-20

a. The Apostolic and Prophetic

i. Foundational

ii. Relational

    b. Deborah's obedience and authority

    c. Called to the Prophetic

VII. God using Women in the 21st Century as Apostles

    a. Apostle Kim Daniels – apostolic attribute personified; anointed for deliverance

    b. Apostle Pernell Hewing – apostolic attribute personified; anointed for prayer

Questions/Discussion/Feedback

Activations – as noted

Conclusion: We have discussed the woman's role in the apostolic move, what it entails, and some of its attributes. As we are led by the Spirit of God, we are not to lean to our own understanding, but in all our ways, acknowledge Him and He will direct our paths **(Proverbs 3:5-6)**, and allow God to do as He wills **(Matthew 26:39)**.

Prophetic Charge (from God 3/7/02):

Daughters, I issue you a charge to rise up for such a time as this to become the women of destiny and purpose that I have called, to help fulfill these end-times; for as I spoke in Joel and Acts, I will continue to pour out my Spirit to fulfill and accomplish all that I have purposed and planned since the beginning of time, Arise, my Daughters, Arise!

I will use all that you have been through and will go through for My glory and purpose to complete and perfect you as my woman of destiny to impact now and the future for my glorious coming back to receive unto me - my Bride, the Church! Be ready, get ready and go forth!

Invitation/Opportunity to Receive Jesus Christ as Savior: Romans 10:9-10

Jesus died for our sins; if you confess this scripture and believe in your heart, you have salvation in Him!

    A- Acknowledge you have sinned; we have All sinned and Jesus died for our sins,

    B- Believe in your heart that God raised Jesus from the dead, and

    C- Confess with your mouth the Lord Jesus, who He is, made the way for your salvation.

Reference Materials: The Bible -King James Version (KJV) and New International Version (NIV)

7 Lessons Teaching Course – "Women in the Apostolic Move"

Lesson I – Apostolic (Apostle)

Objective: to learn **what** the apostolic gift is, its **purpose** and some of its **attributes**

Introduction: we will discuss the current move of the apostolic (anointing) and the Apostle - what it is and is **not**, the restoration of the apostolic gift to the body of Christ, and several attributes of the apostolic.

I. **Apostolic (Apostle): Ephesians 4:11-12:**

(KJV) - **(v.11)** and He (Jesus) gave some, **apostles**; and some, prophets; and some, evangelists; and some, pastors, and teachers; **(v.12)** for the perfecting of the saints, for the work of the ministry, for the edifying of the body of Christ.

(NIV) - **(v.11)** It was He who gave some to be **apostles**, some to be prophets, some to be evangelists, and some to be pastors and teachers, **(v.12)** to prepare God's people for works of service, so that the body of Christ may be built up.

A. **Apostle - Definition/Purpose:**

1. Greek word: **Apostolos** - which means representative, messenger, envoy.

   a. **Envoy** (American Heritage dictionary) - a representative of a government sent on a special diplomatic mission

   b. **Holy Spirit** - one that God appoints to represent Him, and His Kingdom; sent on assignment to do the work He has predestined to be performed.

   c. **an Ambassador** for Christ **(II Corinthians 5:20)**; to have delegated authority to represent the Kingdom of God in a governmental, official capacity, spiritual authority given by Christ with miraculous powers

   d. given power to do signs, wonders and miracles **(Acts 2:43 NIV)**; everyone was filled with awe, and many wonders and miraculous signs were done by the **Apostles**

2. **What it (apostolic) is not** - a missionary **only** (one sent on a mission), usually evangelistic or another specific task. **Apostles** should have an evangelistic anointing, but this is not all that they are called to do.

   Not Limited - an Apostle is **not limited** in the anointing of this Office but operates in the other four ascension gift ministry dimensions (pastor, teacher, evangelist, and prophet) to some degree and at some time or another

B. **Restoration** - movement of God to restore certain major truths **(II Peter 1:12)**; ministry and spiritual experience (signs, wonders and miracles) that have not been widely active since the early years of the Church; to bring back what has not been in operation:

1. **Work of restoration** - to equip, train, and mature members of the Body of Christ **(Eph 4:11-12)**
2. **Last restored**, but first established, set in order **(I Corinthians 12:28)**, **(Matthew 19:30)**

C. **Attributes of an Apostle:** - some are: authoritative, revelatory **(Ephesians 3:5)**, foundational **(Ephesians 2:20)**, to govern and set order in Church **(Titus 1:5, I Corinthians 14:40)**, gather people **(Matthew 12:30)**, build churches **(I Corinthians 3:10)**, reformation **(Hebrews 9:10)**, to finish **(John 4:34)**

Out of these attributes, flow some of these characteristics:

Prayer (Matthew 9:38, I Thessalonians 5:17, Luke 19:1); **Deliverance/Healing** (Luke 4:18, Matthew 10:1); **Evangelism** (Matthew 28:19-20, Luke 10:2, 16:15), and the **Prophetic** (Amos 3:7, Ephesians 3:3-5)

Conclusion: we have discussed what the apostolic is and is not; it's restoration and its attributes.

Questions/Discussion/Feedback

Lesson II – What is her role in the Apostolic?

Objective: to learn the role of **women** in the apostolic move

Introduction: God always had women as part of His plan and purpose from the beginning **(Gen 2:20-24),** and that has not and will not change because there is **no** respect of person **(Eph 6:9b),** God uses who He wants, who is available and ready to be used as a vessel **(II Timothy 2:21)**

II. **Women - their role in the Apostolic move: Galatians 3:28 (NIV),** there is neither Jew nor Greek, slave nor free, **male, or female,** for you are all one in Christ Jesus. Women served with Jesus **(Luke 8:1-3),** were at his crucifixion **(Mark 15:40-41),** first to witness His resurrection **(Matthew 28:1, 5-10)** and with the Apostles after Jesus's ascension **(Acts 1:14)**

A. **God's plan and purpose for woman (Gen 2:20-24), (I Timothy 2:15),** she is the bearer of new life (birth) **(Gen 3:16),** and nurturer (sustainer) of life, helper of man, equal to man, taken from man's flesh

1. **Helper (helpmeet) to man:** (Gen 2:20) - created to help man who has need of help; she is to, help fulfill his purpose in life (ministry), help him live a godly life and become everything he was created to be by God
2. **Equal (taken from his side)** - she is equal in spiritual essence, but different in practical function; taken from man's flesh so she is a part of him - and he needs to cover, protect, and provide for her as the weaker vessel respectively (I Peter 3:7)

B. **God does not discriminate** (or show difference, prejudice) (Galatians 3:28), nor does He have **respect of persons or favoritism** (Ephesians 6:9)

1. **Available, ready, set apart** - God will use whoever is available, set apart, ready, fit for use **(II Timothy 2:21),** and prepared for work
2. **Use** in Greek means **"euchresto"** - helpful or serviceable; person who will be an instrument for noble purposes made holy, useful to God and prepared to do **any** good work (service) **(NIV); Any** good work includes **apostolic** work
3. **No respector of persons** (or showing favoritism)- your Master also in Heaven neither is there respector of persons with Him **(KJV);** we respect

the position, acknowledging a person's position before God as a beloved human being with a divine call and purpose for **(his)** her life, but do not give favoritism to the person

C.   My (personal) position as a woman of God

I have grown and continue to grow in the areas of prayer, deliverance, spiritual warfare, praise and worship, evangelism and prophetic, particularly under an Apostle (apostolic leadership). I have seen the corporate body of believers (in Christ) change, grow and mature in the anointing of God in these areas as well. I am continually maturing and being stretched in areas where I need to grow spiritually and being challenged to become all that God had created and ordained for me **(Jeremiah 1:5; 29:11)**

Conclusion: we as women have been called with a purpose by God and should learn our role in this Apostolic dimension. We have a responsibility to make ourselves ready and be willing to do the work we have been called to do.

Questions/Discussion/Feedback

Activation: What are your roles as a woman? What have you been called by God to do? Are you doing it or need help? In what areas do you need help?

Lesson III – Apostolic Attribute: Power Through Prayer

Objective: to learn the importance of prayer in the apostolic move

Introduction: prayer is our communication with God to talk to Him and hear from Him. For the apostolic move, prayer is of utmost importance because from it, God gives strategies and ways to do things to bring His desired results. Also, we get direction from prayer and need to travail (have an intense desire) in prayer to see manifestation (result). God wants us to pray continually.

(I Thessalonians 5:17 NIV), and Jesus said, "pray and not give up **(NIV)**, or pray and not faint **(KJV) (Luke 18:1)**

III.   **Apostolic Attribute: Power though Prayer: Hannah (I Samuel 1:10, 12-15)**

    A.   **Hannah** was barren (could not have children) and she desired to have a child by her husband. She was taunted by his other wife. After years of this, Hannah decided to try a different and more radical approach to getting what she desired. Year after year, she went to the temple to pray and cry out to the Lord. One particular time, she became desperate and went into reckless prayer where she abandoned all dignity and formality. She was in bitterness of soul, prayed unto the Lord and wept much **(v.10)**, so much so that Eli, the priest, watched her mouth and believed she was drunk with wine because her lips moved but there was no sound for Hannah spoke in her heart **(vs. 12-14)**. Eli asked her, "how long will you be drunk? Put away the wine." Hannah replied that no, I am a woman of sorrowful spirit, and have not drunk neither wine or strong drink, but have poured out my soul before the Lord **(v.15) (KJV)**

        1.   **She travailed** in prayer - "travail" means strenuous mental or physical exertion, tribulation or agony, anguish, labor:

            a.   **Labor** - Greek word - agonizomia - meaning to strive

            b.   **Desperate** desire, reckless abandon - forget formality to go for what is wanted with all that is within you to get the desired result; giving all that you have, leaving it all on the altar

2. Manifestation (desired result) of prayer - **(vs.19-20)** ... and the Lord remembered her, so in the course of time, Hannah conceived and gave birth to a son **(NIV)**

Manifestation of apostolic move - signs, wonders and miracles

B. Prayer releases the apostolic anointing - Jesus encourages us to pray to the Lord to send forth laborers **(Luke 10:2)**

1. **Praying with power and manifestation (Luke 6:12-13)**

Jesus prayed all night to God, and when it was morning, he called His disciples and chose twelve of them to be **apostles (NIV)**

    a. Prayer is the **strength** of apostolic ministry (especially prolonged or all-night prayer, *i.e.,* - prayer watches at church)

    b. through prayer God releases strategies and revelation to get His purposes and plans fulfilled **(Ephesians 3:5)**

2. **Pray continually (I Thessalonians 5:17) and not give up (Luke 18:1)**

We pray and do not rest until the plans and purposes of God are complete; to be tenacious and relentless in the drive to finish (see manifestation); even through resistance or temporary setbacks, continue to breakthrough every barrier until the mission is accomplished!

C. **My personal prayer life** has become more intense, strengthened, and elevated to higher levels in the spirit realm. God sometimes answers quickly and other times answers to prayers are delayed. I may have to wait, but He always comes through! I have a desire to pray for all things, not just some things because God is mindful of everything that goes on in our lives. I start and end my day in prayer as well as praying throughout the day; it is a part of who I am. I do not feel prepared or complete without prayer and cannot live without it. I have learned to trust God for the results and not go on my own or manipulate the outcome in anyway.

Conclusion: prayer is of vital importance in a believer's life, and we should ALWAYS pray and NOT give up!!! We will see the results as God intended if we persevere, hold on and have Faith that what He said and has for us will come to be.

Questions/Discussion/Feedback

Activation: Prayer is a conversation with God – talking and listening (two-way communication); learn to do more listening (Psalm 46:10) than talking. What God has to say is more important anyway. Think about this: there is a reason He gave us two ears and one mouth.

Increase and have an effective Prayer life: Pray the Word of God and Pray in the Holy Spirit (Romans 8:26-27, Jude 1:20)

Lesson IV – Apostolic Attribute: Deliverance

Objective: to discuss the role of **deliverance** in the apostolic move

Introduction: when God wants to use us in an authoritative position that we are **not** even sure we can handle, how do we respond? Do we trust him and obey? Or do we turn down His request because of **fear, doubt, uncertainty, feeling unworthy/insecure or some other reason?** We may or may **not** know the impact our decision to answer the call of God; how it affects us and others. We will look at **Esther** and how she obeyed God in helping to deliver a nation from destruction.

IV. Apostolic Attribute: Deliverance (Esther 4:14) - "For if you remain silent at this time, relief and **deliverance** for the Jews will arise from another place, but you and your father's family will perish. And who knows but that you have come to your royal position [authority] for such a time as this?" **(NIV)**

    A. Esther was groomed and prepared to become the king's wife; had obtained his and God's favor to be in this position at this appointed time. As apostolic people, we must be prepared **(Ephesians 6:10-11)**

        1. Strategize against the plan of the enemy - Esther came together with the Jewish people to fast and decide to go before the king; risk death for their deliverance. **(vv. 15-16)**

        2. Obey and take authority - she was strong and courageous in obedience **(Joshua 1:9)**
believing God regardless of the outcome; was an **ambassador**

    B. Spiritual warfare and deliverance in the apostolic are needed to stand, come against strongholds, the attacks of the enemy **(II Corinthians 10:4-5)** and strategize to see the purposes and plan of God fulfilled

        1. Warfare - Greek word - **strateia or strateuomai** means career, military service (as one of hardship or danger), to **execute** (perform) the apostolate, to contend (battle) with carnal thoughts

        2. Stronghold - Greek word - **ochuroma** meaning a fortress, fortified place; apostolic people have the ability and anointing to confront and pull-down strongholds; strongholds are linked with imaginations (thoughts or logic); we must develop **new** mindsets, be renewed in our minds **(Romans 12:2)**

C. Personally: deliverance and spiritual warfare is very real and as we grow spiritually, we will begin to see and understand how vital it is for us as Christians. We must learn how to war in the Spirit, cast down imaginations and get/maintain personal deliverance. This helps us to be victorious in our spiritual walk with God and stay focused on Him **(Romans 8:7-9)** to fulfill our purpose and destiny.

Conclusion: spiritual warfare is very real for we have an enemy of our souls (the devil), but God has given us the victory through Jesus Christ!! We must learn to war for the victory for the battle is not won with flesh and blood, but through God and His Word. We can do all things through Christ if we are courageous to trust God and obey His instructions.

Questions/Discussion/Feedback

Activation: Deliverance is a continual, ongoing process; we need and should want to be delivered from our past hurts and disappointments, anger, fear, and anything else that is keeping us from being free to do and be all that God has already decided from the beginning of time. **(Jeremiah 1:5)**

What do you need deliverance from?

What is needed to maintain deliverance and not go back to the way before (accountability)?

Lesson V – Apostolic Attribute: Evangelism

Objective: to discuss the role of **evangelism** in the apostolic move

Introduction: we have a great (command) commission from Jesus to spread the gospel (good news) of who He is; and teach all things we have learned of Him. In this lesson, we will see evangelism in team ministry, and the vital importance of souls for the kingdom of God.

V. Apostolic Attribute: Evangelism (Matthew 28:19-20) - Jesus commanded us (as believers and followers of Him), "go therefore, and teach all nations.... teaching them to observe all things whatsoever I have commanded you; and I am with you always, even unto the end of the world." **(KJV)**

   A. Priscilla, along with her husband were taught by and traveled with the **Apostle Paul** to spread the gospel and teach others about Jesus **(Acts 18:18-24);** even to the extent of opening their home **(I Corinthians 16:19)** (Home ministry and bible study)

      1. Team ministry - we are more effective working together than alone; Priscilla and her husband worked together in ministry (and business) which enhanced their ministry **(Deuteronomy 32:30).** God desires that husband and wife stand together as one for Him **(Ephesians 5:31)**

      2. Taught under Apostolic authority - Priscilla was taught by the Apostle Paul and traveled with him, for which she gained experience and growth.

   B. Jesus commanded us to be followers and disciples (learners) of Him so that we can tell and show others who He really is; especially and particularly under apostolic authority - **signs, wonders, and miracles** will follow **(Mark 16:17)**

   C. I have become more **kingdom minded** (about what God wants and how He operates), as well as concerned about the souls of others; whether they know Jesus **and have accepted Him as their Savior and Lord (believed and received).** Not only this initial step but being taught His ways and allowing their lives to be changed for His purpose and conformed to His word. I am concerned about the souls of people I meet and those I haven't;

therefore, I pray for souls to receive Jesus and have eternal life with Him. Wherever we are, we should allow the Holy Spirit to lead us in the opportunity to invite a person to receive Jesus as Savior and Lord. Sometimes a conversation can create that opportunity; one plants, another waters, but God gives the increase **(I Corinthians 3:6)**

Conclusion: Jesus died for souls to receive Him and come into His Kingdom. Evangelism is a mandate from the Master for everyone to reach the lost. We want others to have eternal salvation and avoid eternal damnation; also, to know Jesus to fulfill the purpose and plan of God for their lives.

Questions/Discussion/Feedback

Activation: Do you evangelize? Concerned for the souls of others? Evangelism can be as simple as starting a conversation about almost anything – something that holds another's interest.

Be led by the Holy Spirit, our Helper, Teacher who knows All things.

Have you received the in filling of the Holy Spirit? This will endow you with power to reach others.

Lesson VI – Apostolic Attribute: Prophetic

Objective: to learn how the **prophetic** relates to the apostolic move

Introduction: we will discuss the relationship of the prophetic in the apostolic move; how it is foundational with the apostle. We will also look at Deborah, the prophetess in the book of Judges and how she moved in obedience and authority for God's people to be victorious.

VI. Apostolic Attribute: Prophetic -Amos 3:7, "surely the sovereign Lord does nothing without revealing His plan to His servants the prophets. **(NIV)**

    A. God wants to reveal to us (His servants) His plans, therefore, we should desire to become a prophetic people to hear what the Spirit of the Lord is saying so that we can plan, strategize, and obey what God wants us to do. We are not all called to the office of the prophet, but we should all be prophetic and desire to prophesy. **(I Corinthians 14:1, 3 and 39)** It is of utmost importance to hear from God; **not** only to hear but have the courage to obey.

        1. Foundational (Ephesians 2:19-20)- "... but fellow citizens with the saints and members of God's household, having been built on the **foundation** of the **apostles and prophets,** Jesus Christ Himself being the chief cornerstone." **(NKJV)** They help build the foundation of the church by:

          • Prophets: hearing, revelation, and directing

          • Apostles: authoritative, truth and establishing

        2. Relational: (Ephesians 3: 3-5)- ".... which in other ages was not made known to the sons of men, as it has now been revealed by the Spirit to His holy apostles and prophets." **(NKJV)** God will also avenge them **(Revelation 10:7)** Apostles and prophets have similar anointings and work interdependently.

        3. Deborah - (Judges 4:4-14) she received divine, strategic revelation from God to defeat the enemy of Israel at that time. She also was a judge (authority) of Israel; heard and had the courage to obey for victory!

Deborah - Prophetess, Wife, Judge, Warrior, and Worshipper (Judges 4:4-14; 5:1-31) A woman of diverse giftings; here is a brief summary of her roles. Similarly, we are called upon in this time to fulfill these roles, and with God's help, we can do it also **(Philippians 4:13)**

Prophetess - in the book of Judges, chapter 4, verse 4, she is called a prophetess and received divine revelation from God as to how to defeat the enemy of Israel at that time. Jabin was the king and Sisera was the commander of the army **(v.2)** who oppressed the Israelites. Barak, another judge, and commander of Israel's army was given the strategy to free His people by Deborah. **(v.6-7)** Not only did Barak receive the instructions, but insisted that Deborah go with him to be a part of the rescue mission **(v.8-9)**

Wife - chapter 4, verse 4 also tells us she was the wife of Lapidoth; she lived and worked in the hill country of Ephraim, between Ramah and Bethel. This calls for balance in her life as she devoted time for God, was a wife and performed duties as a judge.

Judge - verse 4 also tells us that she was a judge; a respected woman with authority who settled disputes for the Israelites. This means she had wisdom from God to serve in such a capacity and at such a difficult time in history for the people of Israel; under a system of monarchy when kings ruled. A judge is a position of prominence, respect, authority, and honor.

Warrior- in chapter 4, verses 5-14, she gives Barak the plan and command of God. Barak has such respect for her that he will not go into battle **without** her. She states that as a woman, and in battle with him, he would not get all the credit (honor) he deserves for victory. Barak insists and she goes to assist him which takes great courage, strength, and faith in the word of the Lord. She not only gave the word from God but helped fulfill it and was victorious! She was a woman of obedience.

Worshipper - beginning at verse 1, chapter 5 is called the song of Deborah for she pours out of her heart and spirit to the Lord in praise and worship; not only for who He is but what He has done. She gives Him all the glory and describes how this all came about from beginning to end. The end being the death of the Sisera, the commander of the opposing army, although he believed he had escaped. It is a song of glory and victory! God is praised from beginning **(v.2)** to the end **(v.31)**.

B. My ascension gift is that of the Prophet (Ephesians 4:10-11) - God has called me to this office. It is **not** something I asked for or chose on my own; God does this. As I am in fellowship with God; He is my dance partner in this spiritual waltz. As He leads, I will follow and will not step out of order. He will order my steps **(Psalm 37:23)** and make the way to fulfill purpose and destiny.

Conclusion: Prophecy is a powerful gift from God to reveal His purpose and plans. We want to receive instructions for our life and live out the specific will for our life. God will tell us if we are willing to ask and seek Him for it. It is not only for us, but to help others as well.

Questions/Discussion/Feedback

Activation: Do you have a desire for the prophetic, to prophesy? **(I Corinthians 14:1)**

Do you hear from God? If you want to hear from God, you can be activated

The Conclusion of the Matter: All that we do for the Lord must be in and with His Love **(I Corinthians 13:1-13)**, which is the greatest gift and commandment **(John 13:34-35)**.

Lesson VII – God Using Women in the 21st Century as Apostles

Objective: God is using women in the twenty-first century as Apostles

Introduction: I believe that we are in those last days God spoke of in the books of **Joel and Acts** (our key scripture for this teaching). In this twenty-first century, God has called forth women to be Apostles. There are many women today who are Apostles with the anointings of prayer, deliverance/healing, evangelism, and the prophetic serving in ministry. We will discuss two examples of **today**, Apostle Kim Daniels and Apostle Pernell Hewing.

VII. God using women in the twenty-first century as Apostles (Acts 2:17-18)
God will pour out of His spirit on **all** people … both men and **women** (NIV)

God – personify Himself in women

Personify – (American Heritage dictionary): to think of or represent as having the personality, qualities, thoughts, or movements of a living being; to **represent** by a **human** figure.

Examples:

A. Apostle Kimberly Daniels

1. Apostolic attribute personified – anointed for **deliverance;** the "Demon Buster" who has written books and teaches deliverance with power and authority
2. Ordained by Apostle John Eckhardt

B. Apostle Pernell Hewing

1. Apostolic attribute personified – anointed for **prayer**, Owner of the Sanctuary in Wisconsin, who has written books and teaches
2. Ordained by Apostle Bill Hamon

Conclusion: Yes, God uses women today as Apostles. We are blessed to be His messengers to do kingdom work and must not allow anything or anyone to keep us from fulfilling our purpose and destiny in this Apostolic time.

Questions/Discussion/Feedback

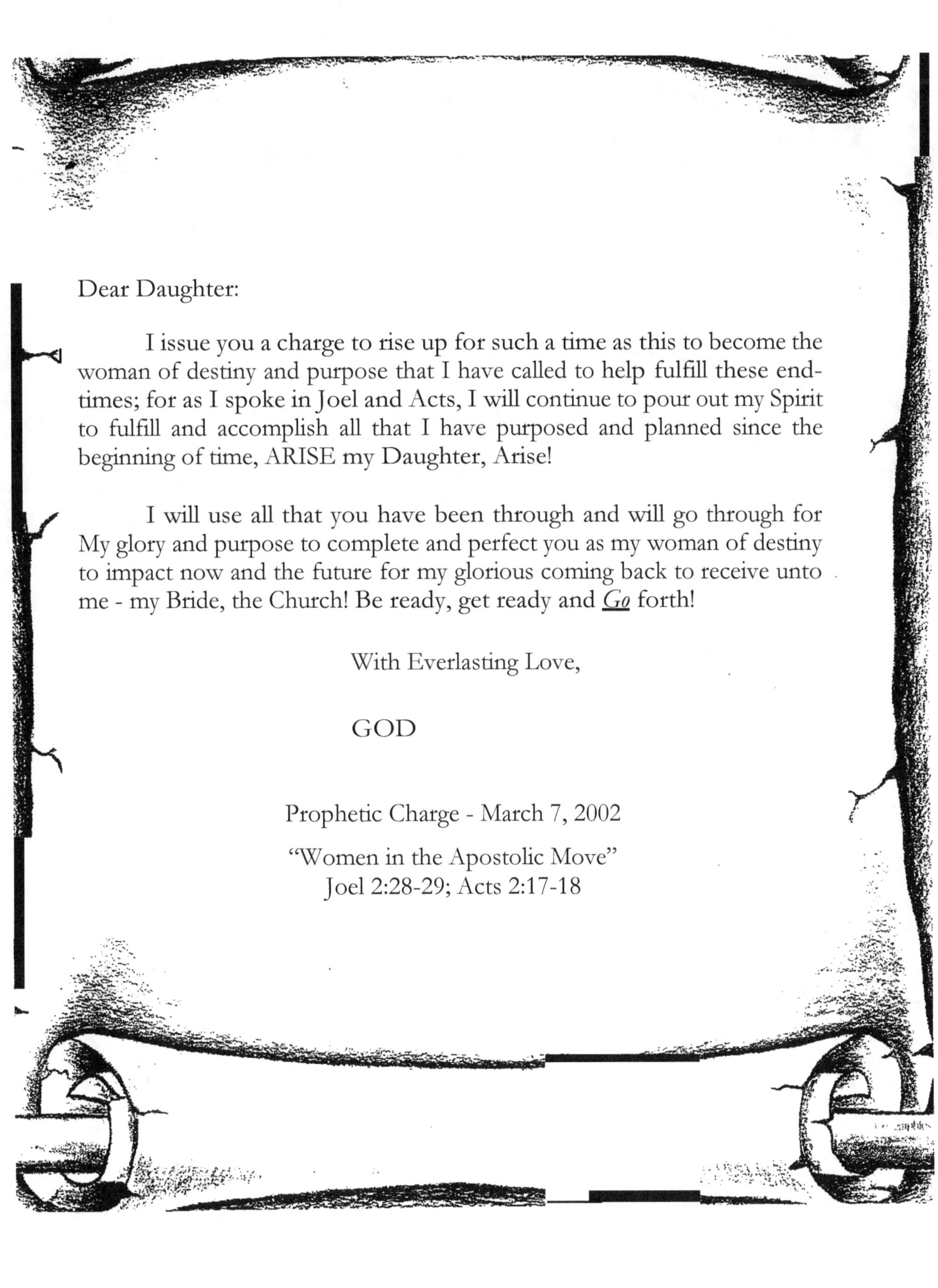

Dear Daughter:

I issue you a charge to rise up for such a time as this to become the woman of destiny and purpose that I have called to help fulfill these end-times; for as I spoke in Joel and Acts, I will continue to pour out my Spirit to fulfill and accomplish all that I have purposed and planned since the beginning of time, ARISE my Daughter, Arise!

I will use all that you have been through and will go through for My glory and purpose to complete and perfect you as my woman of destiny to impact now and the future for my glorious coming back to receive unto me - my Bride, the Church! Be ready, get ready and _Go_ forth!

With Everlasting Love,

GOD

Prophetic Charge - March 7, 2002

"Women in the Apostolic Move"
Joel 2:28-29; Acts 2:17-18

Biography

Rochella O'Quinn is an ordained Elder and Prophetic voice who desires to see God's people healed, whole and restored to fulfill their purpose and destiny. She is the author of *"Lord, I Need Sexual Healing"* – a book to help those who want to be whole, restored and walk in holiness. She has also written *Inspirational poems* from the scriptures.

Teaching over twenty-five years to numerous audiences on various topics such *Hearing the Voice of God, Dreams and Dream Interpretation, Women in the Apostolic Move, Prophetic Evangelism, Holiness, and Faith* has given her the opportunity to reach diverse communities. Her twenty-five years of service to the Kingdom and Body of Christ includes the Prophetic Teacher & Leader, Evangelism, Healing & Deliverance, Prayer, being a Mentor, Armor-Bearer, Singles Ministry Chairperson and Youth Leader.

Rochella has completed external course studies from Moody Bible Institute. She is certified at the American Association of Christian Counselors (AACC) caring for people God's way.

As an accountant, she has over thirty years of accounting and auditing experience as an auditor, supervisor and manager of auditing, grant manager, procurement and budget manager.

In her leisure time, she loves to read and watch sports such as football and basketball.

www.ingramcontent.com/pod-product-compliance
Lightning Source LLC
Chambersburg PA
CBHW08123713 0726
47997CB00009B/2907